ALL ABOUT THE BENJAMINS

CHANGING THE WAY YOU THINK ABOUT MONEY

ANN CAUGHMAN

authorHOUSE

AuthorHouse™
1663 Liberty Drive
Bloomington, IN 47403
www.authorhouse.com
Phone: 833-262-8899

Published by AuthorHouse 12/07/2020

ISBN: 978-1-5462-7664-7 (sc)
ISBN: 978-1-5462-7663-0 (hc)
ISBN: 978-1-6655-0541-3 (e)

Library of Congress Control Number: 2020921029

Print information available on the last page.

Scriptures marked as "(CEV)" are taken from the Contemporary English Version Copyright © 1995 by American Bible Society. Used by permission.

CONTENTS

JUST WANT TO SAY THANKS

A Special Thanks to my daughter...

Joiray Khalfani El, is a wonderful friend and daughter, who is always there to support me and to assist me in whatever I need. She is a supportive wife, a loving and caring mother and a marvelous daughter. I couldn't have asked for a better support team.

A Special Thanks to my granddaughter...

Aniyah Stith, a wonderful young lady who stepped in at the last minute to help her grandmother with the illustrations in this book.

And to those that I have met...

Thank you to all those that I have personally worked next to and who have taken the time to mentor me, encourage me and guide me. You have been an answer to a prayer. You didn't have to do it, but you did. From as early as I can remember, I have been blessed to have had individuals come into my life at just the right time to teach me just the right thing. To the many of you, I say, Thank you.

And to those that I have never met...

I have never met most of my mentors face to face or shared a stage with them or taken a picture with them, but I have met them through their messages, their books, their sermons and their videos. I have sat in their seminars and taken many of their courses both online and off. Although they have never met me or traveled in my circles, they have taught me many things that has changed my life and the lives of my family. To the many leaders in the financial, spiritual, and personal development arena, I say, Thank you

INTRODUCTION

There was a 2002 movie called *All About* the *Benjamins*. It was about the struggle and determination of getting money and the idea of using that money for a better life. The name represents the face on the one-hundred-dollar bill. The characters in the movie went through a lot of battles to obtain money. Their efforts to obtain money went from working at a job that they didn't like, to playing the lottery, which is a game of chance. It occurred to me that for most people, time has not changed the methods that have been used to obtain money. In fact, when I was growing up, long before 2002, the same things were going on. I have learned much about money since then and this book is to share just some of that information. I have had money and I have lost money and I have decided, having money is better. My intent is to lay a solid foundation about money and how it works. In the long run, I trust that this information will inspire you to change how you think about money and to give you the insight on how to use it. It is not meant to give you everything you will need to know but it will point you in the right direction. After all, money is currency and it is meant to flow. It may as well flow to you and through you.

With that said, take note, this book is about money. Pure and simple, money. I've read that money answers all things, so I had to wonder, if people are experiencing so much trouble, or living such average lives and not experiencing the joy and happiness that was intended, could it be that they did not have enough of the answer, which according to this saying, would be money. I've heard so many people say so many times that money can't buy everything. After I thought about it, it was the people that didn't have any money that said it the most. I've heard that it can't buy you love or heal you and it can't make you happy. Money doesn't bring peace of mind or give you a sweet sleep at night. It can't bring anything spiritual or eternal into your life. And you know what, it can't. But then, it wasn't meant to. It was meant to answer all things natural. Do you know what else I've noticed, those who had it, had a better love life, the best doctors to help with their illness, mental or physical and the least amount of worries to cause them to have sleepless nights and a life of stress. So, from what I saw, money did answer a lot of their questions or should I say, solve a lot of their problems.

Now who are the "they". When I was a young adult, "they" used to be the 5% of the people that held 95% of the wealth in the United States. Now, as of a 2013 study, 20% of the population holds 89% of the wealth of America and the remaining 80% of the population holds a whopping 11% of the wealth[1]. Of the 20%, only 1% of the households (considered the upper class) hold 37% of the wealth and 19% (the managerial, professional and small business stratum) hold 52.2% of the wealth[2]. That means the average household, the 80% are the wage and salary workers.[3] In terms of financial wealth, the 1% holds 42.8% of the wealth.[4] We are talking about wealth, not just money. The difference between wealth and money will be discussed later. They, the 1%, are the ones that the average say are the only ones to lead them to the place that they, the average wants to be. I was an "average" and I'm sure my story is not much different than those who were around me. So, from this point on, I will be talking directly to the other "average" 80 percenters, trusting that the information in this book will first change your mind set about money and then give you the courage to make whatever changes are necessary to change your financial position. I know that by doing so you will be able to live the life that having money can give you. I believe that all families have a right to financial literacy and that financial literacy will increase your chances of having the financial success that you desire for you, your family and your business. With that in mind, the foundation for wealth must first begin in the mind of the reader. It will not do you or I any good to talk about budgets, the positive or negative impact of credit card debt or the importance of having a good credit score if you have mind blockers that will continuously bring you back to your starting point. You will be going in circles, getting discouraged and thinking that "It's just not meant for me". "It is what it is." These are statements that I have heard from so many discouraged people. These are not true statements. They are statements of unbelief and discouragement. This writing is meant to put an end to that line of thinking. Yes, you can and should have money and wealth. The following pages will help your soul to prosper and put you in a position not only to receive money and wealth but to keep it. I wish above all things that thou mayest prosper and be in health even as thy soul prospers. 3 John 2

THE WHY OF IT ALL

The biggest most important lesson that I have learned is that it is not about having the money, but about what you do with it and how you think about it that counts. It is what you think about and do with the money that will determine if it will work for you or against you. It is not an easy lesson to learn, but it is a lesson that will change your life and the lives of your children and children's children. Money does not work for the average person, the 80%, it is the average person that works for it. The 1% has learned how to get money and then how to make it work for them. And that my friend, is what I, and I dare say, many of you were never taught. But that ends now. The knowledge that is found on the pages of this book will teach you what the wealthy knows and how to use that knowledge to change the course of your destiny. It contains information that will draw wealth to you and not away from you. This information is not taught in many schools or colleges. It is not taught in most of the homes in the 80% group. It was not taught to me, and to many of you and therefore, we could not teach it to our children. But the time for that is over. I trust that when you gain this information that you do not keep it to yourself but that you teach as many people as possible. Help me to change the course of our families, our communities and the future of generations to come. From this point on, I am going to share with you, and I hope many future generations through you, *All About the Benjamins.*

Have you ever heard anyone say, "You can't take me where you have never been?" Now that may be true for some things, but when it comes to money and wealth and how it works, that's a learned experience. I am very glad that it is. When I looked around my world as a young adult, those that I saw were in the same position that I was. Some may have had a little more and others a little less, but none were where I wanted to go. Therefore, I was at a lost to who was going to take me where I wanted to go. What I wanted was to fulfill the dream that was within me. What I wanted was something more than just the talk of what I heard from the people around me. I, like I am sure most of you, wanted to fulfill the purpose for my life or at least what I thought was the purpose for my life and to be able to give the best to my family. I wanted more than I had. But I had no one to tell me how to get it. One thing I knew for sure was that it was going to take money.

My why began when I was spiritually awakened. There was something within me that moved me to want to do more than I was doing. My call or purpose in life if you will, was to teach first the Word of God and then within that, teach people how to occupy. The first thing I learned was that occupy meant that I was to teach those that crossed my path how to do business, which included business in the family and business in their respective industries. Little did I know that my purpose included many difficult lessons about money. I should have known that I needed to know that because we live in a capitalistic society and money is a big part of it. I've learned what I am going to share with you by trial, error and learning from others. My mindset has changed about money and yours will have to as well if you are not where you want to be. I have learned that money has a purpose too. It is meant to move and to fulfill dreams. It is meant to provide you with the things that you and your family can enjoy. Therefore, it is my purpose to help you put money to work in your life and for you to be able to tell when it is not working on your behalf. When this happens, your lives will be changed and then our communities will be changed. The result is more people in the 1%. There is a transfer of wealth that has begun to take place in the land. The 5% of people controlling the wealth when I was a young adult is now the 20% as indicated in the prior stated statistics. You and I will be in place to receive a portion of that transfer if we can learn and apply what they know. This is the reason for me wanting to know about money. This is my why? You will have to find out your why. And yes, you do need a why.

Why is having a why so important? Knowing why you want to accomplish something or to have something will keep you going forward when things get difficult. There will be obstacles along the way to realizing your dream and road blocks in the way of you reaching your destination. It is your why, your reason, your purpose that will cause you to keep moving. So, take a moment now before you read any further and begin to think about your why. Your real why. Let me help you. Think past the things you want. Think past what you want for your children. Think past the things you want for your business. Believe it or not, the why that is going to keep you is the why that is bigger than you. Think about the things you would do if money was not an issue. Is there anything that you want to do or see done that is bigger than you? Is there something that you would like to see changed and no one is changing it? How about knowing why you feel the way you feel about a certain thing or a certain subject? Is it because your parents felt and thought that way? Is it because you saw or heard something from someone else that moved you to want to make a change? Who set the course for your life? Was it your decision? Your answers to these questions will lead you to know your why? That way when you come to a road block you will not be quick to give up or turn back. You will remember why you started on this journey and furthermore, why you are going to keep going. The reason you keep going will be your big why. Now don't get me wrong, your family and business are also a part of your why. They are the ones that will reap the benefits of your efforts of becoming financially literate and independent. Knowing your why will also help guide you into your what to do and your how to do it. By the way, you cannot truly be financially independent without becoming financially literate. You will see this when we compare income with wealth.

Well, have you given it some thought? What is it that you want to do? Who is it that you want to be? What is your purpose, your calling? I know that this may be difficult. I hear so many times the questions, "I don't know what my purpose is?" or "Why was I born?" or "I don't know what to do with my life?" Questions like these leave an empty place within you that must be filled. The answer to these questions is what will give your life purpose. There are many books and messages out that say they can help you find this purpose. One thing is for sure, without this purpose, if you are fortunate enough to get money, the money that comes into your life will not have a reason to stay. Remember, money is meant to flow. Let me give you an example. I'm sure you know of a similar story. Think about the person that has just won a million-dollar lottery. This person, like the one in the movie, took a chance and won. He or she now has a million dollars. He can say, "I am a millionaire". Now what happens? If he has not figured out his why, after buying the houses, the cars, and anything else that money can buy, he after a couple of years (if that long), will be in a worse place than before he had the money. Why do I say a worse place? He will not have the money and he will most likely be in debt. Even if he paid cash for what he purchased, he did not prepare for the continued upkeep of what was purchased and did not plan on how to keep the million-dollars making more money. Have you ever wondered why this has happened to more than one person? I can hear you saying that this wouldn't happen to you. But how do you know? Have you planned what you would do if you had a million-dollars? Would you know how to invest it for continued return that would benefit you and your family? For that matter, would you know where to invest it? A million dollars does not last forever, if it is not directed with purpose, it will surely go through your hands into that of another. Most likely, it will go into the hands of the 1%.

Let's look at another example that is a little closer to home. Let's take an average person from the 19% of the top 20%. That's the group of managers, professionals and small business owners. Now many in this group has had some experience dealing with money and most of them earn at least a six-digit income. Yet how come more of them are not in the 1% group called the wealthy? Perhaps even in this group there are some things that still need to be learned. The same questions would apply to the six-digit earners. Without a purpose or a mission, if you will, their money will also dwindle away or instead of being transferred into wealth, it will be transferred into debt. This is one of the reasons why knowing the differences between earning income and having true wealth will help you in your journey to financial independence.

We all need to have a why, why? Because no one else can tell you what your purpose is even though they may try to. If you're not careful you will spend years trying to fulfill someone else's dream. There used to be a time when you would get a job and stay there until retirement. The company would reward you for your loyalty by giving you a pension. The time when rewards are given for loyalty on your job are over. As a matter of fact, many companies will drain your youthful years and then try to replace you in the later years. The retirement plan offered by employers today must be funded with your own money. If you think about it, even your employer is telling you that you must take control of your own financial future. There are some companies that will at least match what you put away and you should, by all means, be taking advantage of that.

Let me take a little trip for a minute and talk about purpose. In my studies of the wealthy, I have heard it said many times that you cannot become wealthy or obtain a millionaire status while working for someone else. I have found that this is not true. There are plenty of stories that contradict that belief. For example, I read about a parking lot attendant who saved five hundred thousand through investing and never earned more than twelve dollars an hour, Mr. Earl.[5] He called it nickel and diming it and invested into the stock market by buying a stock here and a stock there, with whatever he could afford. He just did it consistently and on purpose. His why was that he didn't have much education and he was labeled a slow learner, so he dropped out of school in the eighth grade although he went on to get a high school diploma.[6] Remember I said that your why must be bigger than you. Do you want to know the why of Wal-Mart leader Sam Walton? Walton gave value to people above all else.[7] Value to people not to himself or his family. This is an important factor on your journey to wealth. Your why must give value to something or someone greater than yourself. I remember when I was writing our church's millionaire status confession. I included a statement about our money giving value to others and at that time, I did not fully understand why I included such a statement since I wrote it in the beginning stages of my personal transformation. Little did I know that statement is what helped me narrow down the true purpose or vision that was within in. I like what Mr. Earl did with his knowledge and his wealth. He paid it forward by giving shares from his personal portfolio to others and then taught them how to make it grow plus he started an investment club at his church so that others can grow and learn to gain wealth as well.[8] Mr. Earl's actions suggest another type of mentality. Have you ever seen a crab get pulled out of a bucket of crabs? What happens? The other crabs in the bucket try to latch onto the "escaping" crab and one of two things will happen. The escaping crab is either pulled back into the bucket or the "latching on" crab is taken out with the escaping crab. Most times the "escaping" crab doesn't get away because the other crabs in the group latch on to each other. Each one attempting to bring the other one back into the bucket. Thus, you have the metaphor of the "carb mentality". It usually means that a person thinks "If I can't have it, you can't either". You will never rise above your current circumstances with this mentality because while you are pulling someone else down that means that you must stay down yourself. Please remember that when you help someone else to rise, you will rise yourself. You know that saying, "Do unto others as you would have them do unto you." Perhaps, this is clearer, "What goes around, comes around."

Are you beginning to see the importance of having a Why? This is your chance to dream. Let me encourage you to dream big! Have you thought about your future? What you would like to do when you retire? How much money will you need or want to fulfill that desire? Get a vision, see yourself there, write in down. Be very clear and detailed about it. Then run towards that dream and the money will begin to come. It will flow right to the dream. Of course, it will not flow on its own. You will have to direct its path. You will have to make sure that it has a place to go and you will have to make sure that it gets there. Then, it will begin to work for you. Later we will look at what to do with it when it is in your possession.

INCOME: THE ROAD TO WEALTH

It's amazing that one of the most important topics to life is one of the least talked about subjects. Did you know that the Bible has more than 2000 scriptures about money, wealth and possessions and that it's a rarely discussed topic in many of the churches of today? When it is discussed, it is only in relation to giving a tithe or an offering. It's rarely taught how the balance is to be used, invested or put to work. It is like that in most homes as well. Most people are taught to go out and make money but not what to do with it afterwards. Most pay bills, but do not know the importance of paying bills on time. Some are taught to save, but not where to save so that the money they do save will truly increase. The average person does not know the difference between having wealth and getting money and yet, so many say they want to be independently wealthy, financially stable and to owe no man nothing. It would seem therefore that we need to determine what is meant by money or income and wealth.

What is meant by money? Money is the income that is usually received on a regular basis from work or investments. It is received in exchange for goods and services or for labor. It can also come from a return on an investment. A statement that has become

17

common in the financial world is multiple sources of income. This statement means that money is coming from a variety of places. It indicates that money coming from one source is no longer enough for a person to reach financial independence. There are multiple types of income and many sources of income. Although it is not the intent of this writing to go into the details of them all, a few are mentioned so that you can get an idea of just how many streams are available to you. The income that is most common to you is income that you trade your time for. It consists of your wage or salary which includes bonus and incentives, your commission and income from entrepreneurialism. An entrepreneur is one that works for him or herself therefore they are their own employee. This is called active income because you must actively participate in getting it. In other words, this is called earned income. Let me take a minute here to talk about a few resources of income.

Remember Mr. Earl. He let us know that it is not the kind of job that you have that will make you wealthy. I say this because there are some that think that you cannot work for someone else and become wealthy. These next few statements will also help you to identify where your passion may be. There are several major industries of influence in our culture and you may have a passion to work for someone else within one of them or to have your own business within one of them. Either way, your desire may be to become a voice of influence that may result in a needed change in that area. Let's take a quick look at these areas. One industry or area of influence if you will, is government. With all the talk and changes going on today, you may have a burning desire to do something about it. If so, this could be your passion and your way of giving someone value. If so, I encourage you to pursue the dream. I'm not saying you have to be president, you may just have a desire to become an advocate for those that do not have a voice. Do you like to talk? A second source of income can come from the media. Do you wish that there were better choices to watch on television or listen to on audio devices? Perhaps you are talented in this area and always wanted to become a television producer but were afraid to try because someone laughed at you or made you feel bad for dreaming. There is also the entertainment industry. This includes the arts as well. If you are talented in this area you can become very influential. Just remember to get wealth you want to add value to the people that will be watching you. The same goes for the industry of business. You have the solution to someone's problem within you. You could pursue a career in what would encompass small or large corporations and perhaps build relationships of integrity between corporations and the consumer. Building businesses is the ability to create wealth for someone else. Of course, there is the family which is the foundation of our communities. How important would it be for family values to be restored? Are you getting any ideas of where you can do what you love to do and make income too? Are you a teacher at heart? There are numerous ways to change lives in the educational system. The seventh industry is the industry of religion. Yes, even religion is a business or an industry where many lives can be changed for the better. I've shared these things with you to help you see where income can come from and hopefully to help you find your purpose if you didn't know where to begin to look. Work in any of these areas can be a source of earned income. I will dedicate a chapter to these sources of income so that you can understand the workings of each of those industries just in case they become a part of your vision and purpose for you and or your community.

The next source of income that we are used to hearing about is called passive income. Another name for passive income is residual income, unearned income or income that gives you leverage. This is the source of income that most people try to attain when they first begin thinking about becoming financially independent. This income is a result of money that is generated by not working for it. It is money that works for you. It consists of income from real estate, which is what most people think of first, multi-level and affiliate marketing and or royalties. Let's look at one source of potential passive income. Real Estate. There are a number of possibilities to make money in real estate. Of course, the most common is rental property but everyone is not meant to be a landlord. Some other ventures include real estate investment trust (REIT). You can invest in a REIT just the same as you would a mutual fund account. It is a company that holds multiple income-producing properties to which you can "buy stock" and reap a profit. Another type of real estate is flipping houses. In this venture you buy, fix and resale. In real estate wholesaling you are the middle man. You get paid for doing the foot work for someone else as owner. Yet another side of real estate investing is procuring land and houses from the purchase of tax liens. You can see just from the real estate side there are numerous opportunities to make passive income. Other types of passive income can include books which include e-books and audio books. Becoming an author is getting more and more common. It is one of the most common ways you can share your information with someone else and add value to them. When you do, you are on your way to a wealthy place. You can develop online courses as a source of passive income. Once your course is developed and a good marketing plan is in place, your work is done. You can sell your course over and over again without any additional effort. Passive income is also income derived from doing business. Business is income received from someone else's labor and not your own as in entrepreneurialism. In business, you become someone else's boss not just the boss of yourself. The possibilities of generating income are endless. I have had some of my clients tell me that they make money by streaming their video game playing on the internet. There are people that will pay to watch you play video games. Have you ever seen a street sign holder as you were driving by? They are income earners and seem to actually have fun at it. I know at times they make me smile when I drive by. That's added value to me. I am sure they add value to their employers, or they would not continue to pay for the service. When you drive by a sign holder from this day forth, ask yourself, is he making money to invest? You just never know. It's not always what it looks like from the outside.

There are many, many ways to make passive income. You can literally search the internet and get hundreds of ideas to put in place. It all depends on how much time and effort you are willing to put into it. Sometimes, your financial journey will require you to find additional sources of income so that you can save more and that's okay. Do what you have to do to get where you want to go. Remember everyone's situation is different. The destination may be the same, a wealthy place, but the road travelled will be different for each one you.

The last type of income is called portfolio income. This type of income comes from the earnings of the savings that you have invested. It comes in the form of dividends, interest and capital gains on your investments in mutual funds, stocks and bonds or index related savings. It can also include collectibles such as gold, silver, other natural elements and foreign income. This is also called paper investments. In other words, the value is not dependent on any one person working. Portfolio income can consist of works of art, stamps or coin collections and antique items. There are some people that have wine collections. Portfolio income is truly the result of your money working for you. Another way of thinking about a portfolio is to think about it as a multi-sectioned wallet that holds your various unearned income sources or your assets.

People think they know what money is or should I say what money does. You see people who buy a lot of things, that look or dress a certain way or that drives a certain type a car and your first thought is that they must have money. Having money however is not the same as having wealth. Money is the simplest form of wealth. It is the form of exchange for goods and services that is generally accepted. It is also the exchange that will move you from one financial position to another. No matter how old you are when you first become aware of the need for money, you will need to understand how it works and what you can do with it. As a matter of fact, the sooner you learn what money can do and how to do it, the sooner you will move up the financial ladder of success. What is the ladder of financial success? The ladder of financial success represents the transition through the various levels of security to reach financial independence. The details of the levels will be discussed later but for now, know that the road to financial independence takes you through provision, sufficiency, abundance or more than enough, wealth and riches, and finally generational wealth or leaving a legacy. Each person may be at a different step on the ladder at any given time. One must be willing to gain more knowledge and more insight with every step. If one is not careful, they may even fall back a level. How many times have you or someone you know appeared to be doing better and then all of a sudden, you are back where you started and most times, you don't know how you got back there.

In our society, one becomes aware of the need for money at a very early age. Your first contact with the importance of money comes when, as a child, you hear your first "No, I don't have any money." If you can remember your first "No, we don't have enough for that." You can remember how it felt not to have money. Then as soon as you get to be of legal age, you get your first credit card. You didn't ask for it, wasn't sure how to use it and didn't have enough money to "pay" for it. At this point, you and most people, have had little if any form of financial education. You knew that you could use the credit card without having money right then but was never taught that it will cost you much more than what you intended.

Can you remember how you felt when you received the bill and you couldn't pay it and then noticed how the balance just kept getting larger and larger? This is the first experience with money that many people start with and without any financial education, it lays a foundation that keeps most of the people in the 80% bracket having only 11%[9] of the wealth and would usually keep them at the provision or sufficiency stage. It is the use of money in this manner that keeps people out of the wealth class. For those that are fortunate enough to have been taught financial literacy, the wise use of money would put them on the path towards wealth at an earlier stage than most.

Wealth is more complex than money. There are many facets of wealth and it may be different for everyone. Wealth for most people includes things that money cannot buy. For the purpose of this writing, we will be discussing wealth and its monetary meaning. Wealth cannot be achieved without the wise use of money and the knowledge of how it works. Wealth is defined as the net worth of all accumulated assets in your control. Notice I said, in your control. Those that have wealth that consist of a lot of debt do not have true wealth at all. I heard one of my mentors say, "Those that have money only have money if they can spend money." That rang true to me. If you owe most of your money to someone else, you do not have control over that portion of your money. If you do not have control over it then you cannot spend it. If it is not yours to spend, can you really say that you have it? Just think about it. You say you own a car, but most people have a note on it and are paying it off monthly. Do you own the car or does the bank own the car? At the most, it is shared ownership. How about your house, do you own it or is it shared ownership with a mortgage company? If you are renting…well that's enough said already. One of the best ways to see how wealthy you are is to see how long you can live at your current lifestyle after you stop receiving earned or active income. In other words, wealth is not how much you have made, it is very much about how much you have saved. It is not about how much you have to spend, it is about how much you keep. Wealth is about paying it forward. How much do you have left after living the life that you want and doing the things that you were called to do? After fulfilling the purpose of your life, how much do you have to pass forward to your children's children? Each truly wealthy person should be able to leave their grandchildren an inheritance. (Proverbs 13:22) The inheritance should not only include financial security but also the knowledge to keep it going forward to their grandchildren. We should all be two generations ahead to truly be called wealthy.

Before we leave this discussion about wealth, let me talk a little about what it means to be a millionaire or to have financial independence. I have learned that everyone that calls themselves a millionaire, after a closer look, is not a true millionaire. This brings me to the difference between cash flow and net worth. Most people think that it is their net worth that determines their level of wealth. That is not totally true. Now I am not demeaning these teachings because most that teach on this level also teach on the importance of budgeting, restricting your spending, cutting back and having some level of savings. They also teach fix-it strategies to get you out of a hard-financial place but do not tell you that those fixes should be temporary and that there are more permanent strategies that will keep you out of the hard places. All of these strategies are important and most of those that are beginning their financial journey are starting from a place of not enough. They will need to learn the basics of these strategies so that a solid foundation can be laid on which the more permanent, leave a legacy strategy can be built. The purpose of this book is to get you thinking far past the beginning of your journey and to get you to see your self at the leave a legacy stage. As you will see later, if you can see yourself at the leave a legacy stage, you will be able to get through the not enough stage. Let's get back to what it means to be a true millionaire.

I can still hear one of my trainers say, "A millionaire with no money is not a millionaire at all." Wow! How true is that. What he was saying was that most of the millionaires that he had come around only appeared to have spendable cash. They were in debt and what money they did have was tied up into products or assets that were not liquid. In other words, they could not get their hands on their own money when they wanted to. Simply put, their net worth was equal to their assets minus their debts. Since net worth does not consider liquidity, you can have a bottom line on paper, of millions of dollars, and still have no money to buy dinner. Unless of course, you choose to go into debt by using your credit card. Cash flow on the other hand is a true measure of your financial status. Could you write a check for a million dollars? Cash can be considered those funds that you can have access to within 24 hours. Now, some would say, if you have access to your money within thirty to ninety days, then you can consider those funds liquid. But I think like this, if God tells me to help someone in need financially (irrelevant of the amount), I don't want to be in the place to have to say, hold on Lord, let me see what I can liquidate? I want to be able to say, OK, how much and pull out my check book. That's the difference between cash flow and net worth. That's a true millionaire. However, our goal is to get you to what ever level you feel financially independent and, in a place, to leave a legacy whether it be cash flow or net worth. In either case, you want to be debt free and or have only debt that brings a good investment.

Now that we have defined income and wealth, let's see how you can turn income into wealth and create a lifestyle for you, your family and your business. First things first, do you believe that you can become financially independent?

YOU ARE WHO YOU THINK YOU ARE

One of the most thought-provoking pictures that I've seen is of a cat with the shadow of a lion. Dr. Bill Winston said in one of his sermons, "A lion is not the fastest animal...not the biggest...and not the strongest. But he thinks he is." [10] In other words, there are animals that are faster than the lion, bigger than the lion and stronger than the lion but the lion is king of the jungle. What do you think is in the minds of the animals when they see the lion? Do you think the faster animal, like the cheetah, thinks he can out run the lion? How about the biggest animal? The elephant or the Rhino, do you think they ever thought that they could defeat the lion? The same with the strongest animal. The grizzly bear is one of the strongest animals and yet it doesn't attempt to confront the lion. The lion is king of the jungle because he thinks he is, and those thoughts are so strong that he believes that he is. The lion acts like he is king of the jungle and everything around him does too. This picture implies that there is a lion within the cat. I need you to see the lion in you.

Yes, I said I need you to see yourself like a lion. Why? Because I cannot change your situation for you. I wish that I could. But you will have to learn the same lesson that all successful people had to learn, no one can do it for you. You are your own worse enemy. I know, I had to learn it too. How I wished I had someone to guide me and to convince me that it was OK to be successful. I knew that I could but somehow it never happened to the level that I had anticipated. Then one day, the light came on. I realized, and some would still say too late (but I wouldn't), that everything I needed to succeed was within me and only I could get it out. I hope that by the time you are reading this that you have overcome any similar feelings or thoughts. If not, know that it is never too late to change.

These negative, can't do thoughts, don't deserve thoughts, wish I had help thoughts, have been preconditioned into many people by their surrounding environment since birth. They have become known as the paradigms. My summary of a paradigm is a set of ideas, concepts, consistent actions, standards and or thought patterns that have been used to develop one's personality, beliefs and character established over a continuous period of one's life, usually during the ages from birth to about age ten. It is these paradigms or beliefs that eventually turn into mind blockers especially if they are of a negative nature. These paradigms have been imbedded into our subconscious and it is the subconscious that arise unknowingly to cause us to make decisions that can be against our personal desires. These subconscious thoughts come in the form of traditions and are usually passed down from generation to generation. Most beliefs are given to us by our parents and or grandparents. As we became of school age, our teachers knowingly or unknowingly played a big part in planting seeds of negativity within our minds. For example, before school age it was alright for us to use our imagination. We were taught to dream. Questions like, "What do you want to be when you grow up?" were common to young ears and set the stage for great ideas to begin to flow. However, when we began to go to school where our imagination could truly develop, we were told to "stop day dreaming" and to "pay attention". Little did we know that these and similar words became blocks for creativity. They became blocks that would stop many from becoming something that no one before them had become. Did you ever wonder why the first person in a family line to go to college was always celebrated? Why were there no others before the one? Could it be that there was a paradigm in the subconscious that needed to be broken in order for the one to make it through. How many times did one hear "A mind is a terrible thing to waste"[11] or "You can do anything you set your mind to do?" These phrases and those like them changed many a paradigm or caused a paradigm shift in the minds of many successful entrepreneurs. People who thought they couldn't make it, changed the way they thought and then did make it. Those who heard negativity for most of their lives and had a turnaround in their mindset, became successful. The same can and will happen for you. You must consider the beliefs that were instilled in you and if they need to be adjusted, then do so. It's not any one's fault, but it is something that must be adjusted in order for you to continue on your path to success. The negative thoughts that go unchecked or unchanged will undoubtedly inhibit you.

Dr. Amen of BrainFitLife, a website that is brain health oriented has an acronym ANTS which stands for Automatic Negative Thoughts[12]. The automatic negative thoughts enter into our minds regularly. Automatic negative thoughts are thoughts that usually take hold of your day, distract you and keep you thinking that what you want is out of your reach. I describe these ANTS as ANTS that travel across your picnic table and consume all the good food that you have out. That's what negative thoughts do. They consume all the good things that you have imagined. Here are some examples of ANTS: "My arthritis is killing me.", "Diabetes runs in my family. I know I will eventually get it.", "Everybody in my family has high blood pressure.", "That will never change. That's just the way it is", "I don't do math, never have, never will.", "All the women in my family are obese, it runs in the family." I can't do that.", "I don't have enough education to get that job.", "I'll never have enough money to pay my bills.", "I always run short of money." "I can't help it, it's in my genes.", "I get a cold every year at this time.", "My mother said...", "We always did it like that". Have you ever heard any of these statements or something similar come out of your mouth? If so, it's time for a change. It's time to change the way you think about yourself. It's time to change the words that are coming out of your mouth. It is time to change your world. There is a verse in the Bible, Matthew 6:31 that says. "Take no thought saying..." This is a very powerful statement. What it tells us is that thoughts may come into our minds, but they do not become our thoughts until we speak them out of our mouths. The lesson is, don't say what you don't want, only say what you want. You may have heard the saying, God tells us we can have what we say, but we say what we have. Think about it, do you talk more about what you have instead of what you want. This applies even when you don't have what you want or can't see a way of getting it. Listen to all the motivational speakers that talk about being successful. They all use this principle. Listen closely to the things that are coming out of their mouths. ANTS are the negative thoughts that enter your mind. It is these thoughts that we don't want to say out of our mouths. What we want to say is what we really want to happen. For example, instead of saying "I do not have enough money to pay my bills.", say "I have more than enough to meet my needs." The ant is the thought that you do not have enough, the power of the words, I have more than enough, will start to change your world and will eventually bring sufficient funds in to meet your needs. It may be strange to some the way this works, but it is the truth. The more you hear yourself speak what you want, the more you will believe that it will come to pass. The more that you believe, the more ideas and opportunities will come your way to make it happen. You create your world by first thinking you can, then speaking like you can and then doing what you can. You will then become what you think you are. Therefore, if you think you have money and wealth, and you start speaking like you have money and wealth, you will believe that you have money and wealth and money and wealth opportunities will come your way. Some call this the law of attraction or speaking positively. I call it, you can have what you say based on Mark 11:24 in the scriptures. The principle of faith is that faith comes by hearing, and hearing and hearing found in Romans 10:17. The more you speak the more you hear, the more you hear the more you will believe (have faith) in yourself. Thinking, speaking and believing are very powerful principles. There is another saying, I believe Abraham Lincoln is given credit for it, "The best way to predict your future is to create it." Welcome to the world of creation, think, believe, speak. You can do all that you can imagine. Genesis 11:6. Therefore, if you do not like or if you are not satisfied with where you are financially (or in any other area) start creating the world that you want. See yourself there. What does it feel like? Is it crowded? How many different bank accounts do you have? What are you and your family doing with the money that is coming your way. Can you see past your debts being paid off? What does it look like? This is how you begin to see yourself in your future. You must come to believe and understand that as a created being, you are a natural creator. You are a part of the creative power and energy that keeps the universe flowing together. You have the power to make changes when it impacts your world because that same power and energy that keeps the universe flowing resides in you.

Most people find it difficult to see themselves in a place that they are not currently in. It is amazing how powerful the mind is. It has become common knowledge that the mind is like a computer. We hear that all the time. We say that the information from a computer is only as good as the information that goes in. What goes in comes out. Right? Then tell me, why we don't think our minds work the same way since we say that it is like a computer. What goes into our minds is what we will get out of our minds. If you are having a hard time seeing yourself where you want to be, you must ask yourself what have you been putting into your mind? We talked about old paradigms that were planted into our subconscious at an early age. But what about now. If you are reading this book, you are more than likely an adult with hopeful ideas or at the minimum you are curious about how money works and how you can get more of it. So, I ask you again, what have you been putting into your mind to develop the vision of yourself that you have? What goes in really does come out!

I remember when I was a young mother. One of my children was a good student and very respectful. Then I began to notice a change. I could not figure out what had happened or changed to cause a change in grades and behavior. During my meditation time it came to me that a TV Talk show was being watched on a daily basis after school. The show was famous for showing children that disrespected their parents, were disruptive in school and had very poor grades. I was led to stop the program from being watched. By the next semester, this same child had a change in attitude and better grades. What an obvious difference! What goes in really does come out. Another example is with the video games of today. Many of the games that seem to draw the young adults are violent. They call it war games, but the language and story line reflect anything but a legitimate war. Some even represent war in neighborhoods. War against authority figures, people that are angry, people that are different, and on and on. I can hear you saying, "It's only a game." Just remember, what goes in, shooting, killing, cursing, comes out, shooting, killing, cursing. How about Television shows? If you continuously watch television in a given week more than you don't watch it, you will hear yourself begin to speak like what you hear and act like what you have been watching. Ask the people you trust that are around you because you will probably not be able to tell the change in yourself. I say trust because you don't want any more negativity coming at you than you already have. You just need someone to point it out to you in love. If the young adults in your life begin to have some values that are totally off from who they are, take a moment and listen to what they are listening too. Does it encourage them to fulfill positive dreams or have their ears becomes ant holes that lead to the mind? I like to watch action mysteries. A lot of them are gory, bloody and have violent acts of crime. The shows actually give you a visual of these crimes, nothing is left to your imagination. If I am not careful, my night dreams are affected, or should I say infected. My dreams become violent and out of character for my personality. Therefore, I have learned to put a limit on what I watch. Most recently, I have decided that they are no longer a priority in my TV lineup. My focus is more on listening to and watching things that are in line with what I want in my own life or where I want to go. Thinking positive takes work. The ANTS will always be there to "eat away your dream". ANTS can get into your mind by what you hear (ears), see (eyes) and say (mouth). These are the things that block your dreams.

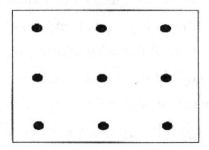

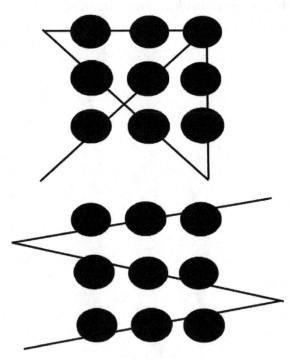

MIND BLOCKERS ARE
MENTAL BARRIERS

Mind blockers are mental barriers to using your imagination and releasing your creativity. When I think of mind blockers, I think about the puzzle with the nine dots. You know the one. You have to draw four straight lines through nine dots without lifting up the pencil. The more challenging solution is to connect the dots with 3 straight lines. The main lesson from this exercise is that sometimes to get the things you want you must think outside the box. Thinking outside the box means you will have to think differently than you've thought before. It also means that you may not have a lot of people that will agree with you. Some of the things that your teachers or your parents taught you may not be applicable for where you want to go. We are talking about using your imagination now, not everything the teacher taught you is wrong. Let's not go to extremes. The point is, if you are not where you want to be, doing what you want to do, to bring in the money that you want or need to have, then you must do something differently and it starts with the way you think. I know I've said that a lot and I hope I've said it enough. Have you ever said or heard these words, "I need a breakthrough."? Stating that you need a breakthrough indicates that there is something in your way blocking you from getting to where you want to go. Sometimes the barrier can be a distraction that will cause you to make a detour from the path that you are on. Sometimes it's something that someone told you that makes you feel like you were not enough, so you gave up. Sometimes it is the fear of rejection because nobody wants to feel rejected. It's just downright uncomfortable to be told no! What ever it is, it is a mind blocker and yes, you do need to break through it. Let's take a look at some of the more common mind blockers. The idea of this chapter is to remove all barriers so that you can let your imagination soar.

Mind Blocker One: I'm too old. You never, ever want to say these words out of your mouth. Who told you that you were too old? Have you limited your life span by the words that you speak? Have you told yourself that you will live to age whatever and now that you are close you think that it is too late? That my friend is the BIGGEST ANT of all times. It will stop you in your tracks. Don't you stop moving towards your goal, you stop that ANT. Your age will not stop you from using your imagination and fulfilling your dreams. If anything, it should make you want to move faster. Remember the story of Colonel Sanders and Kentucky Fried Chicken. He was age 40 when he started frying chicken out of his gas station and 62 when he started franchising his business.[13] It is never too late to reach for your dream. Look around, people are doing it all the time.

Mind Blocker Two: Blurred vision or focus. Perception is everything. Your viewpoint will determine your vantage point. Your perception is your ability to see. When you are in a situation or circumstance you will have the opportunity to perceive yourself from several vantage points. Many people see themselves from the position of hindsight. They understand a situation after the fact. You will hear words like, "If only I had known that before." If in hindsight one considers why the outcome of a situation was the way it was, it will help them make better decisions in the future. Foresight is the ability to predict what will happen or what is needed in the future. This ability is great for limited future mistakes. It means that you must consider the cost and ramifications of your decision before you implement your ideas. This is very important when using your imagination to see your self in a place that you have never been. Foresight is seeing yourself healed when you are sick. It is seeing yourself with more than enough money when you are broke. It is seeing your family united when there is separation. It is seeing yourself as an entrepreneur when you are an employee. Foresight is a powerful form of perception. Another vantage point of perception is insight. Insight is intuition. It is that "gut feeling" or that "something told me" feeling. Insight is acting on thought or idea or concept before it becomes the thing that makes you say, "I knew I should have done that.", when your looking from the hindsight position. Then lastly, perception is eyesight. What you see by means of your natural eye. You must be careful here because what you see with the natural eye can be very deceiving. Have you ever considered why two people can see the same thing and have two different stories? Seeing with the natural eye will make you think you see something that you do not see. That's what makes the statement, "You have to believe it to see it and not see it to believe it.", so powerful.

Mind Blocker Three: Leaving your comfort zone. Leaving your comfort zone is synonymous with drawing outside the lines of the box. Boxes put limits around anything that it contains. Boxes are meant to keep things in one place. If what's in the box doesn't fit tightly you can add to the box to keep what's in the box stable, safe or comfortable, but you can't take what's in the box out. When you stay in the box in your thinking, you confine your imagination and limit your potential. In order to successfully complete the puzzle of the box, you must draw lines that extend outside the perimeter of the box or the content's comfort zone. This is also the place where you trap yourself with the familiar, the place where you begin to criticize yourself. You are disillusioned because everything within you wants out but because you are concerned about what someone might think, you stop yourself right at the edge. In order to reach your next level towards success you must extend yourself beyond the limits of what you know. You must step outside of your comfort zone. With each step you take you get a little more comfortable in your new place. When this new place becomes your new comfort zone, you must again extend yourself and stretch to the next level with the next idea expanding your reach beyond what is easy for you. When you take your eyes off the limits of your box or the boundaries your mind has set for you, when you begin to see from the vantage point of foresight, all that you have imagined will become possible. Set you imagination free. Dare to try something new. Watch new insights, ideas and concepts begin to flow towards you. You will soon see the opportunities for success come your way. They are all just waiting for you on the other side of the boundaries of your mind, on the other side of your comfort zone. Where would you be, if you thought, "What if this works?", instead of "what if this doesn't work?"

Mind Blocker Four: You can't teach an old dog new tricks. Well thank God you're not a dog. You can learn new things every day. As a matter of fact, it is good for the brain. It will take practice, effort and determination but you can make the changes that you need, want or desire to make. I have a plaque on my counseling wall that I refer to quite often. It says "I'm not telling you it's going to be easy. I'm telling you it's going to be worth it." Another saying that I like is "Growth scares people that don't want to change." I say to you, "Don't scare yourself just make the change." I know that many people don't like change. It could be because what you find out about yourself may shake you up a little. Change is uncomfortable only for those that consistently resist it. The more you make changes, the easier change will be. All successful people change. They look for opportunities to make changes because they know that change in some capacity will move you to the next level. At first learning something new will feel "strange" and sometimes even embarrassing, especially when that change must be done in front of other people. But you can break through this barrier if you continue to take one step at a time. Think about it. You have been making changes all your life. It is only as you got older and began to hear things like "I don't like change." or "What's the matter with things the way they are?" or "If it's not broke why fix it.", that you began to resist change. If you are one of the people that say, "You can't teach an old dog new tricks." remember that is an ANT, an automatic negative thought meant to steal your dream. Step on it. If you say that "I don't like change." remember that too is an ANT, kill it. In reality you are a change agent. You made the change going from elementary school to middle school to high school. You've made changes going from adolescence to teenager to adult. You've made changes going from an employee to an employer, from single to married, from unemployed to employed, from manager to vice president. Need I go on? You are comfortable with change, so stop telling yourself you're not.

Mind Blocker Five: I don't need any help. This is a major block that people have when it comes to asking for help. It is a result of being rejected, laughed at or humiliated when you reached out for help. Most times the pain came from someone close to you. Although they may not have hurt you intentionally, they caused you to build a wall that is very difficult to bring down. Seeds of insecurity were planted, and they grew into a sense of false independence. The problem arises because everyone needs help from someone some time. Remember the saying, "No man is an island." You must be able to receive help, give help and work with others. Sometimes your journey may require you to partner with someone to accomplish the task at hand. Never forget that "Team work makes the dream work".

These are only five of many mind blockers. I could write a book on mind blockers by themselves. But I believe that you have enough to work on. Overcoming mind blockers is important when it comes to your income and the welfare of your family. The underlining source of many if not all mind blockers is fear. Fear is the opposite of faith or the opposite of believing that you can accomplish something. Fear is believing that you will fail at doing something if you try. Therefore, nine out of ten times, you will not even try. One acronym for fear is *false evidence appearing real.* Fear will keep you poor. An acronym for poor is *passing over opportunities repeatedly.* Fear then will keep you from taking opportunities that will bring wealth to you and your family. Fear is definitely a thief. The fear of failing will cancel any vision that you have for yourself or your family. But be assured, failing is the pathway to success. Remember, nobody is perfect. Not me, (say what?!?), not you and not even the mentors that we look up to. Without failing we will never find out what truly works. Think of it this way, failure is just trial and error. Every scientist is used to trials that don't work. That's want an error is. It is not necessarily a mistake, it's just not the solution we were looking for. If we can change the way we think about failure, then we will be well on our way to success. Remember, the majority of our society always lifts up the negative over the positive. Just because there were teachers who told you that you failed a test doesn't mean that you are a failure, it only means that you didn't give them the answer they were looking for. So many before us have overcome and changed their thoughts about failure and what it takes to succeed that I thought listing some of their quotes here would be a good summary of how and why we should change our thinking about failure, mental blocks and success because it is a mandatory step in obtaining our dreams.

- ➤ "Failure should be our teacher, not our undertaker. Failure is delay, not defeat. It is a temporary detour, not a dead end. Failure is something we can avoid only by saying nothing, doing nothing and being nothing." – Denis Waitley
- ➤ "I aim for stuff so big, that the dream is bigger than the fear." – Steve Harvey
- ➤ "Everything you want is on the other side of fear." – Jack Canfield
- ➤ "I have not failed. I've just found 10,000 ways that won't work." – Thomas Edison
- ➤ "Step out of the history that is holding you back. Step into the new story you are willing to create." – Oprah Winfrey
- ➤ "Most great people have attained their greatest success just one step beyond their greatest failure." – Napoleon Hill
- ➤ "If you believe you can, you probably can. If you believe you won't, you most assuredly won't. Belief is the ignition switch that gets you off the launching pad." – Denis Waitley
- ➤ "Nothing in life is worthwhile unless you take risks. Fall forward. Every failed experiment is one step closer to success." – Denzel Washington
- ➤ "I can accept failure, everyone fails at something. But I can't accept not trying." – Michael Jordan
- ➤ "...And now nothing will be withheld from them which they have imagined to do." – Genesis 11:6 KJ21

IF YOU CAN DREAM IT –
YOU CAN HAVE IT

Most everyone has an idea of what a dream is. More commonly, it is the movie that is played in your mind while you are asleep. You can see this movie while you are a sleep and it is therefore also called a night vision. Day visions are possible too. Have you ever seen yourself doing something that you haven't done yet? For example, have you seen yourself or pictured yourself sitting on the beach when you knew you would be on the beach in the near future? Have you ever anticipated a good steak dinner (or whatever your favorite meal is) and saw yourself putting on the A-1 sauce? We don't think much about those small pictures. It just seems to happen naturally, like seeing yourself drive that blue Jaguar that you've had your eye on. But suppose you could dream, another way of saying imagine, yourself working the job that you've always wanted, driving the car you've always dreamed of or seeing the balance in your portfolio that you thought you could "never have". One of the things that I want you to take notice of about imagining something is that it is always in the now. It is working, driving, seeing. These all describe things that are being done in the now. That is very important because that is the key to making your dreams or your visions come true. Seeing what you want to have or where you want to be in the now is an important step in the process. In other words, you have to see the end while you at the beginning.

People are making vision boards to help capture their dreams on paper. This is a good way for you to develop your vision. The vision captures a still picture of the movie or dream that is playing in your head and then puts it on a board so that you can look at it continuously. Write the vision, make it plain so that when you see it you can run and plan the route or steps you need to make it happen. I made my first vision book over thirty years ago. It was a photo album with all of my then desires, wants and dreams. I have received nearly everything in that book. By the way, I haven't let go the vision of the remaining items. My dreams today are on a much larger scale and I have a vision wall. Yes, I said wall, so that I can see them (more than one) every morning when I wake up. It helps to remind me of my purpose and my "Why". When I started my vision book it was considered to be "out of the box" because it was something that many people considered to be new age. I am grateful for the few pioneers, although unpopular for their out of the box ideas, stood out of the box and shared it with others like me who were hungry for a better life. They did not have a crab mentality. They freely shared their ideas and concepts and pulled quite a few of us out of what could have been a mundane lifestyle. We did not have a crab mentality and we shared so that others could change their lives for the better. (This is another reason for writing this book, to share what I've learned.) Today people are having vision board parties. There are vision board entrepreneurs who have turned making them into a lucrative business. Another out of the box idea that resonated with me was rap music in the church. Oh My Gosh! I remember almost being cast out of the church. If looks could kill! I would be long gone. Now, look at what's happening today. Rap music, live bands, flashing lights and people are still going to church and loving the Lord. What an out of the box concept! I shared these things so that you will freely allow yourself to dream. Use your imagination. Dream big. It's okay to be different. You may be the one that has the next big out of the box idea.

Visualizing is dreaming on purpose. It is just like producing a movie. When you visualize you are putting the scenes of your life (your goals, your vision) together the way you want to see them manifested in the real world. Taking the time to visualize is meditating on your goals, purposes and your expectations. The biggest difference between you and a producer when you are visualizing is that you are also the actor/actress. This is what makes it real. Now I know that this may sound strange to some of you, but you have used this method subconsciously before. Do you remember seeing yourself finishing school, buying a car or a house? Do you remember seeing yourself in a certain dress or with a certain mate? Come on, I know you have. You were visualizing. The athletes do it all the time. They see themselves winning the game. They hear the cheers. They feel the rush. This is how it works for most successful business people as well. When visualization is done correctly, it will change old self-destructing beliefs and replace them with new "I can do anything" beliefs. Please take visualization seriously. The benefits of meditation or visualization are tremendous. The most import benefit is that it will connect you to your future now. Think about the movie Back to the Future. Visualization will bring your future back to your present. When you begin to dream on purpose you will activate the Law of Attraction and the things that you need to fulfill your dream will begin to find their way to you. When you begin to see things happening for you, you will be motivated to do more. You have to get emotional with your vision. Without your emotional contact the vision won't seem real and the impact will begin to diminish. It is best to see yourself in your dream as often as possible. The more you see yourself successful in business, successful in school or with more than enough money, the more you will believe it and feel it. You will give thanks for it before you even see it because you will know without a doubt that you can and will have all that you can imagine. Remember, visualization is preparing your brain to receive the real thing. When the real thing is manifested, you will be more comfortable in pursuing your out of the box ideas because you have been practicing them during you meditation time. By the way, this process will work for anything that you want to change in your life. You can rid yourself of fears, rejections, poverty mentality and anything else that is holding you back. You can have what ever you say, so please, start saying what you want not what you have.

I won't take the time here to walk through the actual meditation process. There are plenty of books and videos that will take you through the process. The key is to be relaxed and to know what you want. Write your goals and affirmations out. I like to record mine in my own voice and replay them so I can hear myself talking to myself. I find this very helpful. You must find what works for you. Don't fall for the ANT that will come and tell you that only crazy people talk to themselves. I know people laugh when that statement is made but there is nothing funny about it. You better talk to yourself so that you can tell yourself what you want. If you don't you will always be doing what someone else is telling you to do. What I will tell you is that people with crazy wealth do talk to themselves. Read the book "What to Say When You Talk to Yourself" by Shad Helmstetter, and then decide who is crazy. But whatever you decide, get started now. Listen to motivational speakers on YouTube. Listen to positive affirmations of peace, success, wealth and riches. There are literally hundreds out there in cyberspace.

UP UNTIL NOW AND AFTER

Up until now we have discussed the things that impact us on the inside. We covered what we needed to know about ourselves, our plans and the importance of knowing why we want what we want. We should understand what our reasons for pursuing wealth are, and that those reasons must be bigger than our own personal gain. We talked about how what we think about ourselves will have a direct impact on our actions and the creation of our world. We become what we think about ourselves. We took a look at the things that would prevent us from accomplishing the things that we wanted. We understand that there are mind blockers and mental barriers that have been taught to us from one source or another. We realize now that we must breakthrough those barriers that would keep us trapped inside a box. We understand that in order to be successful and to fulfill the dreams and visions that we have for ourselves that we must become comfortable with doing things outside the box. We must also be willing to go outside the box alone as many are fearful of things that they are not used to. We must be willing to let our imagination be stretched so that we can have the next big idea. We now understand how we have been programed since childhood to allow certain automatic negative thoughts to enter into our minds and inhibit our financial growth. We now know that we can stop those ANTS from eating up the great ideas that are within us. We know that we have to see our future self in the present now, not tomorrow, not next year, but now. Our future is now. We are the makers of our own dreams. We know that if we can visualize it, we can have it. We can create our own future.

By now, our soul should be prospering or at least we should understand that this is the first step to having physical prosperity which is health, wealth and wisdom. We know that this book will be discussing prosperity as it relates to money and wealth. Up until now, your soul which is your mind, will and emotions have prospered. You are ready to move to the next level of "AFTER". After your mind, will and emotions have been set towards prosperity, you can safely learn how to get and keep money without money getting and keeping you. Now I know that my soul has prospered and that I am ready to receive the wealth that is needed to fulfill my dreams. Take a thoughtful look at your mind, will and your emotions, and ask yourself, do you have what it takes to get to the next level?

Before I go on, let me dispel a few myths about working for money. There was a time when one would get a job and keep that job for 20 or more years so that one could retire with a pension. This was also the time when staying loyal to one employer was considered honorable and if you left your job for another job too many times, you would be considered an unstable employee. Please permit me to shed some light on these misconceptions. One, most jobs no longer have pensions to give away. What they have to offer is the opportunity for you to put your money into their managed account. Secondly, if you considered your job to be more than just a resource that provided you income, you would notice that staying on one job and most likely in one position, even if you moved up to a managerial position, would limit your knowledge to that of the position or industry that you were working in. Consider this, do you like the job you're doing? I have heard so many people say that they don't like their job, but they stay there because they "need" the money. Many people have been money driven for many different reasons and they miss out on many opportunities that would prepare them for their true purpose and place them in a position to amass true wealth. This brings me to another painful realization. Many people claim not to know their purpose. They have no idea why they were created and what they should be doing with their lives. When asked what they would do with a million dollars, the only thing they can think of is to buy what money will buy, or worse, say "I don't know." When people become older or something goes wrong on their job and they are forced to leave, then some will attempt to think about what they really want to do while others will just find another job that they don't like. People will also mistakenly conclude that the only way to amass wealth is to become an entrepreneur. Then they enter into another source of work and they don't understand that instead of working for someone else, they are working for themselves. They become their own employee. They also find out much too late that they will end up working harder and making less money because they have not obtained the knowledge or the discipline that they need to work alone. Did you ever notice that the first type of entrepreneurial business that people try is the business that they were doing when they were working for someone else? What gets me is that since they didn't like it when they were doing it for someone else, why they think they would like it for themselves. After all, people who say they don't like their jobs also say they like the people that they worked with. This is the normal reaction when a person is trying to break out of the old and into something new.

I don't want you to think that working for someone else is a bad thing. It can be a very rewarding experience and it could be where you are supposed to be. What I do want you to understand is, if that is your "calling" then embrace it and move to the top of that field. Remember, it is not the money that brings wealth, it is what you do with the money that will bring you wealth. One more comment about money. It is understood that everyone does not want to be a millionaire. A million dollars is just a seven-digit dollar amount. What is important is that you get and sustain the amount of money that will fulfill your biggest dream and last you at a minimum through your lifetime. Some may amass and be satisfied with a few hundred thousand dollars and others will go on to amass a few billion dollars. It's your dream. I am here to help you dream without limits. You are in charge of setting your own boundaries.,

In the next chapters, in order to help you determine what your purpose is or where you fit in, I will discuss the four different

Cash Flow Quadrants as explained by Robert Kiyosaki.[14] This will also help clarify the most traveled income journey. From here, you will be able to determine if and when you should be working for someone else, for yourself or have other people work for you. There is no right or wrong answer. All successful people have gone through all the quadrants at some point in their journey. The discussion is meant to help you identify where you are in your income journey, where you need or want to be as it relates to your dreams and perhaps shed some insight into your why. I will also talk about the major industries that have been established in our society to help trigger what you are passionate about. This will help you determine your purpose. Your decision about the kind of lifestyle you want for yourself or others and the industry that you want to be a part of, will help you develop your dream job, your dream lifestyle and your dream for your community. All these pieces together will give your money a purpose. It is at this point that money will actually begin to flow into your hands. Don't forget we talked earlier about how money is meant to flow. With a purpose or mission, you will attract a money flow so that it can it can get through you, to accomplish the goal that will benefit someone else. While it is passing through you, you will find that you will have more than you need to fulfill your personal visons for yourself, your family and your business with plenty left over. So, let me ask you, "How big can you dream?"

After the income journey comes the wealth journey. I share the road most traveled to help you determine where your journey will begin. We all start in different economical levels. It is not a good thing or a bad thing. It is just where you are. Once you determine your starting point you can determine the best path to take you to the next level. This level will start at provision and move to generational wealth and legacy. It is impossible to include all the information that you need on these pages. So, keep in mind, the purpose is to open your eyes and to get you started on the right path.

THE INCOME JOURNEY: TO WORK OR NOT TO WORK

The title of this chapter indicates that we have a choice in the matter of working. The truth is we don't. Every person works in one capacity or another. Each person, including you, can and does choose how much work, how hard to work and most times where to work. You can also decide if you want to work for money or have money work for you. When Mr. Kiyosaki explains his Cash Flow Quadrant, he has described what I am calling the income journey, the road one travels from employee to investor. Mr. Kiyosaki's program consist of four different people with four different mindsets at different levels in business. Let's look at each area that Mr. Kiyosaki describes as the ESBI concept. When you look at the quadrants, there is some general information that you should make note of.

Employee: You have a job	**B**usiness Owner: You own a system
Self-employed: You own a job	**I**nvestor: You own investments
If you are an employee or if you are self-employed: • you exchange your time for money • you have no control over your time • you have no leveraging power • you fulfill the dreams of someone else • you are a part of the 80% This does not apply to you if you are doing what you are called to do in the industry that you are in and you are making a change that will impact lives. Then you are fulfilling your dream or using your job as a source of income to fulfill your dream.	**If you are a business owner or an investor:** • you have control over your time • you have leveraging power • your income is not dependent on your presence or you actively working • your money is making money (passive or residual income) • other people are working on your behalf • you are a part of the 1%
Based on Robert Kiyosaki's Rich Dad's Cashflow Quadrant & My personal insight	

Quadrant E and S: Employee and Self-Employed

The left side, the E & S side represents those workers that have linear income. This is the active income that I spoke about in an earlier chapter. This group's income is determined by how much activity they put in. On this side of the quadrant the workers do not have any power to leverage. Simply put, financial leverage is the power to use one financial activity to increase the rate of return on other investments. One whose primary source of income is generated from this side of the quadrant can truly say, time is money because they must transfer their time for money. If they do not give up time, they will not receive income. It is in the E quadrant where you, like most people start. This is usually the first source of income where you become an employee working for some one else. This is the place where you help someone else fulfill their dreams. On the income journey, I consider this ground zero. In this quadrant you feel secure because you have a steady income and with all things being equal can depend on a paycheck. In this quadrant however, you will pay the highest percentage in taxes and receive the lowest amount of benefits paid by others. As an E employee, you must abide by your boss's rules. He or she will limit how much time you can spend with your family by limiting how much time you can take off of work. The S worker is a self-employed employee. The main difference between the E employee and the S employee is ownership of the job. They both must work. Employee E has a job working for someone else and employee S owns the job and works for him or herself. Under the S quadrant you have some freedom on how to use your time, but you are still under the transfer of time for money syndrome. In this case, if you do not work, you do not get paid. In addition, unless you have financed your own benefits, you do not have any paid benefits. As a tax preparer with many new self-employed workers, I can tell you, most do not pay for benefits for themselves right away. This side of the quadrant is where the average 80% of the population resides. They hold only 11% of the wealth. [15]

The 80% of the population in this quadrant is the average person. They are average because they have not been taught much about financial literacy. Remember, most people started out with an imagination that was used to dream about things that would be done in the future. They did not have to be taught how to use their imagination, it came naturally. Then the surrounding voices began to condition them to what society said was success. Get a good paying job, stay there until retirement and stop using your imagination. Now with much information about financial literacy available the imagination and hope of success is growing again. The employees are desiring to be their own bosses and are moving into the S sector. To be successful in the S sector one must acquire additional knowledge and a different set of skills. Eventually, the successful self-employed person's desires will drive them to want to expand and continue to grow financially. This will take them to the right side of the quadrant. The side where, wealth will begin to truly grow.

Quadrant B and I: The Business Owner and the Investor

On right side, the B & I side represents those who have decided to have their money work for them. This is residual income which includes passive income. This group's income is determined by their knowledge of investments and their willingness to seek after financial freedom. On this side of the quadrant the investors pay the lowest amount in taxes and have the most leveraging power. Quadrant B of this side represents the Business owner. In this case, the owner does not work for himself or for anyone else, but he has a system in place so the others can work for him. In this case, it is the people that are generating the income not the owner. On the investor side, Quadrant I, money is generating money. This occurs when you have learned how to make money work for you. The right side of the quadrant represents the 20% of the population.

The investor quadrant is the 1% of that 20% that hold the major part of the wealth and has total freedom of time.

I am glad that I am transistioning into area B. It is an adjustment moving from one quadrant to another as the mindset is different in each area. You must take the time to learn what is required in each quadrant to be successful. It does not come naturally. Success in any quadrant is a learned experience which requires time and effort along with trials and failures and the willingness to change. Can you understand why the first part of the book is so important? I called it soul prosperity but it is this force and change in mindset that will cause you to press forward while on this income journey. The most difficult transistion occurs between the S type and the B type. This is difficult because both leaders believe that they are owners. However, the S type owns a job and the B type owns a system. The S business is dependent of the S owner but the B business is dependent of the B's system. The owner of the S business is limited to the time, space of the owner and is not duplicatable. On the other hand, the B owner is free to come and go as desired and because the system is duplicatable, the owner does not have to be available.

The income journey is summarized as follows. The E type is an employee who has a job. The S type is the self-employed who owns a job. The income from both is considered active and is summed up as no work, no pay. Usually, one moves from the E type to the S type. Following the S type is the B type. This is a business owner that owns a duplicatable system and has people to work for him to carry out his plan and purposes. The I type is a result of knowing what to do with money and how to leverage it and time. Each quadrant has its own mindset and each person willing to go through the process must become aware of the differences. It doesn't matter the order in which your income journey takes, or if you have to go through all of the quadrants. What does matter is that you must master the skill set and have the mindset of each area to be successful in that area. Going through each area will allow you to gain the knowledge necessary to build big business and every big business has a system that can work on its own.

THE WEALTH JOURNEY: TO SPEND OR TO SAVE

As stated earlier, the mindset of the wealthy is different. Being rich is having a lot of money. You can be rich and broke at the same time because all the money you get goes right out into expenses. Remember the lottery winner that spent the million dollars and was in a worse state than before he had the money. It was due to his spending habits. Being wealthy is defined as how much time you can live your lifestyle without working. The wealth journey takes you through a proper wealth sequence.[16] The sequence has five levels starting with the provision stage and moving through sufficiency, abundance, wealth and riches and ending with generational wealth and riches. These will be discussed in detail shortly. Another difference between the the rich and the wealthy is what each thinks about expenses. Let me remind you that what matters most when it comes to money is not how much money you can make and spend but how much money you can make and save. In the income journey you moved from one quadrant to the next by how much money you made either by working for money or having money work for you. However, on the wealth journey it's not about how much you make but more about what you do with what you make. This is called money management or better still, cash flow management. Since spending your money has a great impact on your savings, let me take a minute to discuss the various types of expenses. This will help you make wise decisions as you are on your wealth journey.

There are four main categories of spending that I want to share. First let me say that all spending is not bad spending. Garret Gunderson, in his book, "What would the Rockefellers Do?" made the statement that his system would "eliminate your destructive expenses, manage your consumptive and protective expenses, and increase your productive expenses".[17] Let's see what is meant by these various types of expenses.

A destructive expense is money spent on items that will destroy your way of life and negatively impact your way of living. These are losses that will never be recouped. They include insufficient bank charges, money spent on gambling and other vices as well as payday loans. This spending may cause you to miss financial opportunities and therefore will lead to poverty instead of wealth. Remember what the acronym "poor" stands for, passing over opportunities repeatedly. These expenses should be eliminated from your cash flow plan (budget) immediately. The next type is consumptive expenses. This is just what it sounds like. This is the money that is consumed on lifestyle. You wear this money, eat this money and drive this money. This is what you spend on vacations or the movies. This is money that is spent on enjoying money. Be aware however, that the only return on this money is the joy of enjoying it. It is usually spent on depreciable items and therefore will add no value to your income or assets. The third type of spending is protective spending. This spending is good spending. This is the expense that provides protection for your life and your property. Unfortunately, it is the most overlooked expense and yet it provides peace of mind and a sense of happiness.[18] It can also include 6 months of liquid savings which will eliminate the need to worry when the unexpected things in life begin to happen. The last type of expense that I'll talk about is the productive expense. This is another source of good spending. It is meant to increase your assets and increase your cash flow. This is an expense that would be considered an investment because the expected rate of return is greater than the cost of the expense. Expenses in this category include the cost of education, contributions to the church or other not for profit organizations that you are interested in, and anything else that will enhance your life now and in the future. This type of expense will not purchase things that will disappear. These are the things that you always want to be aware of as you begin your wealth journey. It is imperative that you know your starting point so that you can devise an appropriate plan to take you through your journey. Now lets talk about the levels of wealth.

The first stop on your journey is provision. At this level, you may need help from an outside source. You do not have enough to meet your needs and you are more than likely living from paycheck to paycheck. You are either an employee or you wish you were so that you can have a steady income. But remember, you do not need a shortage of money to be in want. Sometimes, you might make enough but spend too much. Take a look at your spending and see if any of it is destructive. If so, start eliminating this type of spending first. This level is one of the most difficult ones because pride will keep you from receiving the help that you need. If you are not focused you will become desparate. In addition, in this season, you can easily become stressed and full of worry. It is during this season that you need to build yourself up. Listen to inspiration information and anything positive that will tell you no matter what it looks like, you can make it! This is detrimental to your survival. Guard the gates to your mind. That would be your ears, eyes and mouth. Remember what goes in will come out. You cannot afford to let any ANT come and take over your thought life. The struggle is real but it is also temporary. While you are battling the ANTS, you must also evaluate your position. You must be honest with yourself even if it hurts and it probably will. Your goal is to get back to ground zero by any means necessary. If you are in the provision stage you are living above your means. Don't beat yourself up over it. Recognize it, say ouch and make adjustments. Remember not to talk about what you do not have or cannot do. "I don't have enough money." "I can't find a job." As long as you say words like this, the chances are slim to none that you will have enough money or that you will find a job. Since you have the power to create, when you speak, all the universe is going to work to bring to past what you say. Be very mindful of the words that are coming out of your mouth. Cut back where you can cut back, find work where you can find work and receive the help if it is offered but do not go into debt. If you can imagine yourself with enough to meet your needs, enough to meet your needs will be drawn to you. It's the law. When you get through this place of provision, you will arrive at a place called enough.

Enough is having a sufficient amount to meet your needs. This level is called the level of sufficiency. In this season, all your bills are paid and you are not in lack. Be careful though, you still may be sitting at the end of the month waiting for your next check. It can be deceiving because the pressure is off. You may think you have more than enough but you don't. Keep a close eye on your day to day spending. It can easily slip out of your hands. At the level of sufficiency you may think that you're in a position to help someone but you won't be. Anything out of the ordinary, a flat tire and no spare, anything you may have forgotten, your child's field trip that you didn't pay for yet, or something as simple as getting a cold and needing cough medicine can set you back. This is also the area where it becomes easy to take from one bill to pay another, while you're waiting on that next paycheck. Again, be honest with yourself and keep a close watch on your spending. Think about where you are going. Did you write out your vision? This is the time you must keep it before your eyes, in your ears, speaking it out of your mouth because you can easily forget that you are on a journey with a destination.

This is also a good time to "see" where you money is going. It's hard to write things down when you feel like you don't have anything to write down. Especially when you're in the not enough stage of provision. But now, you should be able to write out where you money is going. Don't assume you know. Write it down. If you think that I am asking you to do too much, you do not understand money and you are not ready for wealth. Writing it down also gives you the chance to see your increase. If you don't write it down, any increase will quickly be spent before you even realize that you had it. Trust the process. This is one of the rare times, that seeing is believing. Be aware the he that is faithful with little things, will be faithful in much. During this time, you should talk to yourself each time you go to spend your valuable money. Some questions to ask yourself are:

1. Do I want or need this item?

   a. If it is a need, ask yourself is there any available money (not assigned to another bill or item) left to get it? If not, make a way to save for it. If yes, get it. Make sure it is a true need for something required prior to your next paycheck. In the future make note of future needs by planning for them as they become known.
   b. If it is a want, ask the next question.

2. Is this a must have?

   a. If it is not a must have, stop and do not purchase it now. If you do, it will be emotional spending. Emotional spending is what gets you into debt.
   b. If it is a must have, is there available for money for it? If so, get it, if not save for it. Most times, after 24 hours, the must have will no longer be a must have.

Although this is the level of sufficiency you should be preparing to move into the next level of abundance. Decide how you want to break down your money before you get it. Percentages work well, especially for the person that does not have a definite dollar amount coming in. You have heard the saying, pay yourself first but has anyone ever told you how or how much? Now don't panic, everyone is different, and everyone had to start somewhere. Some of you are paying yourself first and you are not aware of it and then there are those that know they don't pay themselves first. Paying yourself first is a financial strategy that benefits you when you least expect it. You will know that you're reaping the benefit when you hear yourself say, "I'm glad I did that." Paying yourself first includes putting money away for your future in some type of savings account or retirement plan. It also includes creating an emergency fund and a savings account to be used for future purchases. Paying yourself first means putting this money away before you pay your monthly expenses or make any discretionary purchases. It won't be easy to make this adjustment, but it will be worth it. Start with small deposits and eliminate expenses that you can do without.

At this level you come to a place of rest but the fears of going back to not having enough will attempt to contain you and cause you to become covetous. You must become determined to change the way you think about your position and you must begin to speak like you are already at the next level. You must set your mind on abundance. Here are a few statements that will help you determine which mindset you are working with.

- ➢ Poor thinking people say, "I can't afford it"
  Rich thinking people say, "How can I afford it?"
- ➢ Poor Mindset: Do not know what they want to be
  Wealthy Mindset: Keeps a "to be" list
- ➢ Poor Mindset: Have a sense of entitlement
  Wealthy Mindset: Have a sense of gratitude
- ➢ Poor Mindset: Watch TV everyday
  Wealthy Mindset: Reads everyday
- ➢ Poor Mindset: Talks about people
  Wealthy Mindset: Talks about ideas
- ➢ Poor Mindset: Criticize others
  Wealthy Mindset: Compliments others
- ➢ Poor Mindset: Blames others for their failures
  Wealthy Mindset: Accepts responsibility for their failures
- ➢ Poor Mindset: Fears change
  Wealthy Mindset: Embraces change
- ➢ Poor Mindset: Buy now. Pay later. "What's in it for me?"
  Wealthy Mindset: Save Now. Invest Now. "What's the return on my investment?"

Deciding where you are will help you make proper adjustments to get to where you want to be. You must decide if you want it, then if you want it bad enough to make changes. The changes you make on this level will smoothly take you into the next level in the wealth journey. The level of abundance.

The level of abundance is where most of the average 80% reside. These are your professionals which include the working managerial staff, the doctors, lawyers and the successful entrepreneurs. In Mr. Kiyosaki's Cash Flow Quadrant they would be the higher E's and S's. At this level, you have more than enough to meet your needs and to meet the needs of others if it pleases you to do so. It is during this abundance stage that you begin to put your goals in place to make the visions that you should have been writing down begin to come to fruition. Your savings plans should be in place and funding should be automatic. Some things that should be in place include life insurance and if done correctly, this should be a primary savings source. The right life insurance will make you a banker. The earlier you start this process, the more you will have in your bank.

You can be the Banker

Here's another mindset note: A poor mindset thinks life insurance is about death and therefore invest in it too late if at all. A wealthy mindset knows that it is about living an abundant life and makes it one of their primary savings vessels. Other important sources are your emergency funds and retirement funds. These things should be in place outside of your job and under your personal care. After all, it's your life and your money.

The danger of this level is becoming addicted to a consumer lifestyle. The deceitfulness of riches will attempt to cause you to spend on depreciable items over sustainable items. You will want more clothes and shoes than you can possibly wear. You will want an expensive car while you are still paying rent instead of having a rental property and a paid off car. Each financial decision you make no matter how small will impact your financial future. Think things through and determine if they are taking you on the journey towards your next financial goal. Now I understand that everyone doesn't want to have wealth and riches. I personally do not understand why when there is so much needed in this world. I also haven't been able to figure out how someone is going to leave anything worth having to their grandchildren without having more than what they need for themselves. However, for those that want more than abundance. The next level is wealth and riches.

I know that most people think that wealth and riches are the same thing. But there is an important difference between the two. Both mean that you have a lot of money. Remember the lottery winner millionaire that I talked about in the beginning? The winner of the lottery was rich but not wealthy. How do I know? Because when the money was gone, the lottery winner did not know how to get it back. The wealthy on the other hand knows how to get money to make money so that if ever the riches were lost, it could be made again. Let me say it this way. The rich get richer. They do this not because there is anything special about them. It is because they use the knowledge that they've learned about how money works. You will have to do the same. Hopefully from reading this book, you have a different way of thinking about money and the change in thinking has caused you to make a change in your actions. The change in actions has caused you to make a change in your habits and a change in your habits will eventually lead you to your destiny. Mahatma Gandhi is given credit for outlining the process that your beliefs go through to get you to your destiny. That process starts from beliefs to thoughts to words to actions to habits to values to destiny.

At the wealth and riches level, those that are in Quadrant B and I, must maximize the two most valuable commodities, time and people. Both time and people are converted into money when used properly. (Side note: Don't get offended because I said we use people. Your boss is using you to carry out the job that you were hired do to. Only a poverty minded person would think that I meant using people in a negative way. You must really begin to think differently so that these kinds of statements won't prevent you from hearing what needs to be heard to get you where you want to go.) Ok, again, your most valuable commodities are time and people. The statement time is money has a value to it. People have value to them. That's why you can pay someone $20 per hour and pay another person $40 an hour for the same job. It is not always the job that dictates the payment it is the person that dictates the payment. At least it is when they know their value. This is also the level where strategic decisions are made to impact not only your generations but also the community and other people's lives. You are continuously increasing your investment portfolio so that your money is growing exponentially. At this level you feel a sense of gratitude that you can truly experience financial freedom. The things that you must be concerned about at this level is the risk involved in making your assets grow and maintaining a certain level of increase. This frame of mind continues into the next level of Generational Wealth and Riches.

Here is where you prepare your grandchildren to receive what you have worked for and learned. This is the transference of wealth to the next generation. At this level your time is used to continually learn, equip and expand what you have already established. Then it is to be taught so that your legacy will not be wasted or loss. Can you see why it is important to change your mindset? Another mindset nugget: Poor mindset: Holds information and data from others. (crab mentality) – Wealthy mindset: Shares information and data with all who wants to know. (helping hand mentality). This is the last stop on your wealth journey. Welcome to financial freedom at its best.

BONUS CHAPTERS

I understand how important it is that you must know your why for wanting financial freedom. It is this why that will keep you going when you want to give up. It is this why that will help you to stay focused and be willing to come out of your comfort zone. There are so many people that tell me that they just don't know their why. They are not sure what they should be doing or even what they like to do. When I ask about their passion, their answer is "I don't know". When I ask what they would do if money wasn't an issue, they say that they don't know or come up with such a little dream that they could do what they said with a couple of their paychecks. Remember your why must be bigger than you. You know that it is bigger than you because there is absolutely no way that you can even conceive of a method to get it done. You will have a no way, no how mindset about it. When you can dream a dream that big, then you have a reason for money to begin to flow to you. I am going to talk about the seven major industries in our country in hopes that as you think about these industries something will trigger within you to make you either so passionate or so angry that you want to do something about it. When that happens, you have found your purpose. And yes, you can have more than one.

The second bonus chapter will give you some ideas on some of the available types of investment sources that have growth potential so that your money can go to work for you. What you read here is not meant to be any kind of investment advice and I am not endorsing one vehicle over another. My purpose is to bring to your attention some possibilities that you may not have been aware of. The rest, invest or not to invest, is solely up to you. Get a pencil and paper and begin to write whatever ideas come to mind as you begin to read these next two bonus chapters.

FINDING YOUR PURPOSE: SEVEN MAJOR INDUSTRIES

There are seven major industries in our society which can influence lives. There is no greater place to find your why than within these seven spheres of influence. They have always been around, and they have always influenced people but until 1975, no one had named them or grouped them together as areas to be infiltrated as a world changing strategy. In 1975, Campus Crusade's Bill Bright and Youth With a Mission's, Loren Cunningham came together and concluded that to bring a change to the nation, these seven spheres (or mountains as they called them) had to be reached.[19] I agree. Our culture has been influenced by people at the top of these major industries for so long that they have made the uncommon, common. In order to change what this nation is becoming someone must be willing to occupy the high seats within each of these industries and maintain their integrity and morality. If you don't like what is being shown on television, help to change it. If it troubles you what is going on in our school system, help to change it. If you think there are issues within the forever changing family make-up, help to make a change. There is plenty to be done but not many willing to do it. Your purpose is embedded in one of these industries. Find it, pursue it and watch all your needs, wants and desires be fulfilled just so you can fulfill your ultimate purpose of helping to change and or influence one area of the marketplace. You, my friend, have a purpose and yes, it is bigger than you can imagine. You were created to represent someone greater than you on the mountain top. No fears. It is already laid out for you. Follow the process.

> *In the future, the mountain with the LORD's temple will be the highest of all. It will reach above the hills; every nation will rush to it. – CEV (Contemporary English Version)*

The future is now. The Lord's temple are the people with the heart of God that loves the world enough to make a change in the area that they are drawn to. These seven areas of opportunity are summarized below. They are not in any particular order and all the areas are important. As you read through them, let your heart and imagination soar.

ARTS & ENTERTAINMENT

The Arts and Entertainment world is one of the most, if not the most influential industry that one can be a part of. This area is important because it feeds our faith and our actions and are belief system. It includes the music we hear which goes into our ear gates. It includes the things we see on television and mainly on the big screen and stage which go into our eye gates. Both together determines what comes out of our mouth and forms our world.

Can you see the importance of this industry or this mountain and how easy it is to form what we accept as a society? Filmmakers, movie or music producers all have an impact on our culture. Actors, Actresses, Sports personas, all have the power to change our culture. Look how social media has impacted the world. It is not just the young adults or children that have changed their values. The values of their parents have been impacted as well. This has also been called the mountain of celebration[20] because of the euphoric state that the music can bring a person to. Many people have gifts and talents that can be used in this industry. However, to win in this area one must have a strong spiritual or moral foundation to avoid the pitfalls of sex, drugs and alcohol. This negative aura will deceive the wisest person and will eat away any money that would have been used for good.

MEDIA

Media is very similar to Arts and Entertainment except that it also includes the written materials. Newspapers and the news stations on television tend to be forces that have swayed even the political or government arena. The difficulty with this arena is that you must be honest and be willing to be impartial when it comes to reporting news. If you are troubled by all the deception and half truths that is being reported in this media, then yes, this is for you.

Ann Caughman

GOVERNMENT

I do not know where the idea of the separation of church and state came from, but it should not have been. There is a real need for gifted people in the government. Those that can truly be fair and who have a pure heart. Those that have no other purpose than to serve the people can truly make a difference in this industry. Those that are willing to become an advocate for those that need a voice. There is room at the top of this mountain. There are laws that should be changed. I know that there are some that are reading this who would have gone in this field but was told they should not. If you have always wanted to enter into this industry and was afraid to, you may want to reconsider. This could be where your purpose and your blessings reside. Search you heart. Come out of the box. I'm not telling you the road will be easy, but it will be worth it.

RELIGION

Yes, religion in an industry. There is believed to be a superior being in every society.[21] The spiritual battle that exist for this industry is strong. It is a battle that can only be truly fought in the supernatural. If you therefore, have an unction to this mountain top, go for it. You will not be going alone.

FAMILY

The family is the foundation of every community. It is the breakdown of the family that has caused much sickness in the community, both mentally and physically.[22] There is much help needed in this industry. There are so many influences coming against the family unit. There is an outrageous number of fatherless children. Divorce is tearing families apart at an alarming rate. There is truly a need for healing in this area. Therefore, if you are called to this area, come with an extreme amount of unconditional love because you will have your work cut out for you. The pain that is a big part of this industry will not outweigh the rewards that will come. Therefore, whether it be counseling, foster care, social work, day care centers or any other idea that may have an impact on family life, the door of opportunity is wide open.

EDUCATION

There was a time that education institutions were meant to serve as places of training and admonition in the fear of God.[23] Can you remember the times when the Bible played an important part in the education of our children? Harvard University was one of the leading educational institutions that played a major part in keeping biblical values into education.[24] As time went on and the leaders of the school system changed, so did the rules that governed our children. Can you also see the difference in the school environment? There is much more violence in the hallways and the interest of the student body and of the teachers appear to have vanished. There is truly a need here. There are many opportunities in the educational industry, in and out of the school system. Is your creativity meant for this arena?

BUSINESS

Although Business is listed last here, it is the foundation on which all the other industries must rest on. Business is the industry that controls the flow of resources into the other areas. This is a difficult place to be because you must be able to stand against the spirit of money. This means that money should not be the deciding factor for most of your decisions. Wealth is created in this industry. This industry is the basis for the economic systems of the world. It is where the law of supply and demand is at its best. Business includes the marketplace, from the small farm to the largest corporation. It is enterprise, the freedom to pursue and finance any dream or vision. There is so much to be said about the business industry, but the purpose of this writing is just to open your eyes to opportunities within each industry.

These seven industries are the places where money can be made. It is your choice, and the opportunities are endless. If you think about it, there should never be a place where you would have to be unhappy at work. With so many opportunities available, money is literally there for the taking. The right combination of income and knowledge can and will lead to wealth. It is not necessarily how much you make while working, it is what you do with it that counts. With that said, the final chapter will be a short summary of some of the financial tools that will help your money grow and eventually have your money working for you. It is up to you to put your money in the right place to receive the return that you want. Remember the parking lot attendant who nickel and dimed his way into a half a million-dollar portfolio. If he can do it, you can too! Wisdom is the principle thing and with all your getting, get understanding.

These seven industries are the places where money can be made. It is your choice, and the opportunities are endless.

TYPES OF FINANCIAL INVESTMENTS

Before I list some of the investment vehicles that are available to you for financial growth, let me state that there will be no financial investment advice stated or implied, no intent to sway you in any one direction and or no promise of a return. This information is strictly for information purposes to encourage you to take a hands-on interest in your own personal financial life. There are financial professionals available in every state if you want to talk to someone in detail about you specific situation.

The first thing to know about investing is to determine how your investment will make money for you. That means you must know the "Rule of 72". Basically, the Rule of 72 will tell you approximately how many years it will take for your money to double. The formula is simple: 72 / interest rate = approximate number of years your money will double. Here's a simple example to give you an idea of how the rule of 72 will work for you or against you.

Rule of 72		
Years to Double	Invest $1,500 @ 6%	Charge $1,500 @ 18%
4	-	-$3,000
8	-	-$6,000
12	$3,000	-$12,000
16	-	-$24,000
20	-	-$48,000
24	$6,000	-$96,000
36	$12,000	-$768,000

The Rule of 72

Note: A $1500 deposit into a 6% savings account will double in 12 years giving you $3,000. However, that same $1,500 on a 18% credit card doubles in 4 years, so that after 12 years (same as your savings), you will owe $12,000. Now imagine if that were $10,000 or more. When your financial status begins to increase, you will easily have $10,000 to save and will probably have access to a credit card with that much of a limit as well. That's what it means when someone says, "You do the math." Which do you prefer?

TYPES OF INVESTMENTS[25]

Here are some of the investment instruments that will typically be found in a portfolio.

OWNERSHIP INVESTMENTS

Real Estate: This includes any real property that you buy, rent or sell. It usually excludes your primary residence.

Stocks: Represents partial ownership of a public company that will give you a return from their profits in the form of a dividend.

Business: This is a venture that you put your time and money into expecting to make a profit from a product or service.

PRECIOUS METALS & COLLECTABLES: Although referred to as an alternative form of investment because of its liquidity, collectables are owned. This includes anything that in not considered legal tender and has value that someone else is willing to pay for. It includes gold, silver and other natural metals, diamonds and other natural stones, famous art work and rare furnishings and items that have stood the test of time.

LENDING INVESTMENTS

CDs: A CD is a type of savings account that you have committed to loan to a bank for a fixed interest rate and in exchange, the bank has given you a promissory note.

Bonds: This is another type of debt investment (like a CD) but instead of loaning to a bank, you loan your money to the government or to a corportion for a fixed interest rate. There are various types of bonds that you can have.

Cash and Cash Equivalents: This is money in its physical form which is 100% liquid and in its "cash on hand" state, earns no interest or money that is in a money market account or another type of deposit account (savings or checking) which earns so little interest that it is considered cash. Although not advertised as such, your cash when deposited can also be considered as loans since a bank usually has the right to borrow it from you and loan it out to someone else.

ALTERNATIVE INVESTMENTS:

LIFE INSURANCE: I've included life insurance as an alternative because most finanical professionals are not privy to the value of this investment unless they are directly familiar with it and have been taught how it works. It is however, the next best thing to cash, so much so, that if used correctly, it can become your own personal bank[26] with great tax advantages.

OTHER REAL ESTATE INVESTMENTS: *Real Estate Investment Trusts* (REITS) is a venture where income is earned as a third party by working with real estate companies that earn profits from their real estate investments. This may include investing in the purchase or ownership of the real property or the mortgage that secured it. *Tax Liens* are a type of investment where the right to collect back taxes with interest from the owner is purchased. This type of venture has the possibility of turning into real estate ownership.

COMMODITIES: These are investments in resources that are eventually converted to a form to be consumed. For example, food consumption products or oil and energy products would be considered commodities. Another name for commodity investments are future contracts.

VENTURE CAPITAL: This is investment into start up companies for a return of the expected profits.

FUNDS: Funds can be made up of a variety of investment vehicles that have been grouped together. All of the following are various types of funds which you may have heard of: Index funds, Mutual funds, Hedge funds and Exchange Traded funds.

Any and all of these vehicles can be used to fund your portfolio and help grow your wealth. As you reach this place in your journey, I suggest that you gain wisdom of where you decide to invest your money and understanding on how that vehicle works. One thing that I have learned is that the wealthy know where their money is and they know what it is doing.

PUTTING IT ALL TOGETHER

If you have read this book and followed along as I have taught you how money works and how mindsets and thought processes have come about, you now have enough information to want to change the way you think about money. Money is a necessity in the culture in which we live. Although many have been taught that it is not important, that has just not been the case. The fact that we live in a capitalistic society indicates that it is important. Many dreams have been quenched because of a wrong mindset and the feeling that money is out of the reach for many. This is just not the case. Hosea says in Hosea 4:6, that God's creation perishes for a lack of knowledge. I know that many have spiritualized this to mean only in the knowledge of spiritual things, but a lack of knowledge in any area means destruction or to be without. No matter what a person's situation is or how it got to be that way, everyone can have money and or wealth at whatever level one wants it, if they have enough knowledge and is willing to apply that knowledge.

My heart's desire is that your dreams have been reborn and your desire for that dream has been rekindled and your determination has been ignited to such an extent that you are up and ready to run to fulfill it. You are up and on purpose, pulling down mind blockers and mental barriers and killing the ANTS that are trying to eat away the very thing you were born to do. You are up and consistently and diligently seeing youself successful, feeling the joy that comes with that success. You are writing down your dreams and meditating on how to accomplish them. You are seeing yourself walking the dream, talking the dream and living the dream. Your life is changing. You are up and seeing your children fulfilling their dreams. You can see your bank account getting bigger and bigger. The spendable cash is available to take you on your dream vacation, to build up your community, to help the helpless and to encourage others. You can do this. Start your journey to increase your income and to obtain your wealth. So, remember all those ideas that you had and pursue your dreams. The money will come. After all, IT'S ALL ABOUT THE BENJAMINS.

Mr. Money gives Mr. Idea the thumbs up!

IN THE HANDS OF THE PEOPLE

It is important that this book gets into the hands of the average 80%. It is the information in this book that will set the stage to change generations and to have an immediate impact on those communities that need it the most. I am therefore asking you to help me spread the knowledge that is contained in this book. No one is a crab that should be left in a bucket. Help me to help them by putting a copy of this book in their hands. Although there is no age limit to obtaining wealth or when to start, the earlier you start, the more benefits you will reap. Teach your children at an early age so that they can reap more benefits. But no matter what the age, it is important to just get started.

I am available for teaching seminars, conferences, workshops for small and large groups.

Based in the Jacksonville, FL area, you can reach me at: financialanswers@cfaith.com

In case you wanted to know, Ann Caughman has nearly 50 years of business experience and over 20 years of formal education which includes:

*45+ years as a Tax Preparer *35 years as a Business Bookkeeper and Accountant *10+ years as a Retirement Benefit Analysis *8+ years as a Certified Marketing & Business Consultant *25+ years as Real Estate and Mortgage Broker/Consultant *2+ years as a Certified Tax Compliance Specialist for Non-Profits *15+ years in executive management positions *5+ years as an editorial assistant *27+ years as an Ordained Pastor, Inspirational and Motivational Speaker, Counselor and Educator with a *Bachelor of Arts in Economics (Business) & Accounting & English Writing *Bachelor of Religious Education *Master of Religious Education *Master of Christian Counseling *Master of Professional Counseling *Registered Mental Health Counselor all seasoned with a life-time of ups and downs, failures and successes ending with victories that have made all the trials worth it.

The statement "Yes, you can.", is real! Go for it! Now is the time. Do whatever you have to do to accomplish your dream and reach your goals and overcome every obstacle that stands in your way.

Knowledge is power. Power is money. Money answers all things (natural).

WORKS CITED

1 G. William Domhoff, <u>Who Rules America: Wealth, Income, and Power</u>; WhoRulesAmerica.net, http://whorulesamerica.net/power/wealth.html (retrieved July 4, 2018) p. 2

2 G. William Domhoff, <u>Who Rules America: Wealth, Income, and Power</u>; WhoRulesAmerica.net, http://whorulesamerica.net/power/wealth.html (retrieved July 4, 2018) p. 1

3 G. William Domhoff, <u>Who Rules America: Wealth, Income, and Power</u>; WhoRulesAmerica.net, http://whorulesamerica.net/power/wealth.html (retrieved July 4, 2018) p.2

4 G. William Domhoff, <u>Who Rules America: Wealth, Income, and Power</u>; WhoRulesAmerica.net, http://whorulesamerica.net/power/wealth.html (retrieved July 4, 2018) p. 2

5 Owens, D. (2014). *nickel and dime your way to wealth, wealth building on any income* (Anniversary Edition ed.). Columbia, MD: Owens Media Group LLC kindle location p. 25

6 Owens, D. (2014). *nickel and dime your way to wealth, wealth building on any income* (Anniversary Edition ed.). Columbia, MD: Owens Media Group LLC. Kindle location p. 92

7 Sinek, S. (2009). *Start with Why: How great leaders inspire everyone to take action.* New York, New York: Penguin Group (USA) Inc. p233

8 Hill, M. (2016, August 13). Parking Lot Attendant Saved $500,000 and Only Makes $12 Per Hour. Retrieved 2018, from Wealth Motivation: <u>https://www.wealthmotivation.com/ parking-lot-attendant-saved-500000-and-only-makes-12-per-hour/</u>

9 G William Domhoff, <u>Who Rules America: Wealth, Income, and Power</u>; WhoRulesAmerica.net, http://whorulesamerica.net/power/wealth.html (retrieved July 4, 2018) p. 1

10   Wilson, Dr. Bill. (2018). There Is A Lion In You! Raise It Up! USA: BuildUr Faith. Retrieved from https://www.youtube.com/watch?v=R_PiistOlPE&t=2423s

11   Demby, G. (2013, June 15). *News Ads Still Warn A Mind Is A Terrible Thing to Waste.* Retrieved from NPR Code Switch Race and Identity, Remix: https://www.npr.org/sections/codeswitch/2013/06/14/191796469/a-mind-is-a-terrible-thing-to p.1

12   Amen, D. (2018). *Strengthen Your Brain Anytime, Anywhere.* Retrieved from BrainFitLife: https://mybrainfitlife.com/

13   Biography.com Editors. (2014, April 2 last updated 4/27/2017). *Colonel Harland Sanders Biography.* Retrieved from Biography.com: https://www.biography.com/people/colonel-harland-sanders-12353545

14   Kiyosaki, R. (2014). Robert Kiyosaki's Cash Flow Quadrant. Retrieved from KnowledgeBringsMoney.com: https://www.knowledgebringsmoney.com/cash-flow-quadrant.html

15   G. William Domhoff, Who Rules America: Wealth, Income, and Power; WhoRulesAmerica.net, http://whorulesamerica.net/power/wealth.html (retrieved July 4, 2018) p.2

16   Excel Church. (2018). Pathway$ A Financial Literacy Program. Retrieved from Excel Church: http://excelfl.org/pathways/index.php

17   Gunderson, G. B. (2016). What Would The Rockefellers Do? Rip Water, LLC.

18   Gunderson, G. B. (2016). What Would The Rockefellers Do? Rip Water, LLC. p44

19   7 Cultural Mountains. (n.d.). Retrieved from http://7culturalmountains.org/

20   Enlow, J. (2008). The Seven Mountain Prophecy Unveiling the Coming of Elijah Revolution. Creation House.

21   The Seven Mountains of Societal Influence. (n.d.). Retrieved from General International: https://www.generals.org/rpn/the-seven-mountains/

22   Enlow, J. (2008). The Seven Mountain Prophecy Unveiling the Coming of Elijah Revolution. Creation House.

23   Enlow, J. (2008). The Seven Mountain Prophecy Unveiling the Coming of Elijah Revolution. Creation House.

24   7 Cultural Mountains. (n.d.). Retrieved from http://7culturalmountains.org/

25   Wong, K. (2015, February 5). Two Cents; The Many Different types of Investments, and How They Work. Retrieved from Two Cents: https://twocents.lifehacker. com/the-many-different-types-of-investments-and-how-they-w-1683582510

26   Gunderson, G. B. (2016). What Would The Rockefellers Do? Rip Water, LLC.